Night & Day Animals

Written by Emily Bone

Illustrated by Nina de Polonia

Designed by Zoe Wray and Helen Lee

Seasons consultant: Zoë Simmons
Reading consultant: Alison Kelly

The sun sets and the sky slowly
begins to get dark.

Lots of animals are
getting ready to sleep.

Crows find a place to
rest for the night.

Some animals are
just waking up.

Owls hunt for
food to eat.

Short-eared owl

Badgers sleep underground in burrows called setts. They come out at dusk.

They scratch and sniff around.

Baby badgers are called cubs. They play together.

Some badgers clean the sett.
They drag out dirty bedding,
then carry in clean, dry grass.

They hunt for bugs and
plants to eat.

Crab apples

Worm

Bats wake up just after the sun
goes down.

Mexican free-tailed
bats sleep in caves.
They fly out in
big groups.

Moths are also awake at night.
Bats hunt the moths.

Silkmoth

Painted tiger moth

It gets darker.

Owls make sounds to tell other
owls that they're nearby.

Screech owls make
a screeching sound.

Screech!

Owls hunt for food through the night.

Barn owls catch small animals. They feed the animals to their chicks.

Young rat

Fish owls catch fish from rivers.

Trout

There are lots of animals awake
in towns and cities at night.

Raccoons search for food
that's been thrown away.

Red foxes hunt for small animals.

Rat

Opossums go from place to place,
eating any food they can find.

Babies cling onto their mother's back.

Some bugs are only awake when it's cooler at night.

Slugs have wet, slimy bodies that need to be kept cool. They eat plants.

Cockroaches scuttle around at night eating what they can find.

Fireflies are little beetles. They can make their bodies light up.

They flash their lights on and off to find partners.

Hedgehogs sniff out bugs to eat
under plants and leaves.

Baby hedgehogs are
called hoglets.

Sniff!

Snail

Hedgehogs are covered in prickles. A weasel tries to attack a hedgehog.

Weasel

The hedgehog rolls up into a prickly ball. This protects it from the weasel.

Leopards hunt for food at night.
A leopard hides in long grass.
It watches impalas.

Impala

Leopard

It waits for
an impala to
pass close by.

The leopard rushes up to the impala
and bites its neck.

The impala dies. The leopard drags
the impala up into a tree and eats it.

Deserts get very hot during the day but cool down at night. Many animals wake up.

Desert hairy scorpions hunt bugs.

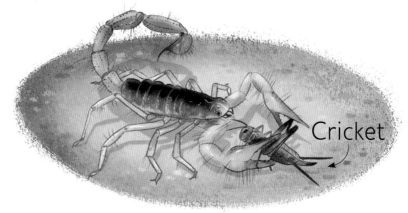

Cricket

Jerboas have very long legs. They can run away from attackers.

Eagle owl

Jerboa

Fennec foxes sleep in cool burrows during the day, then come out at night.

Some stay by the burrow to look after young foxes.

Others hunt for food.

Mouse

Many parts of Australia get very hot too.

Koalas sleep in shady trees. They wake up at night to eat leaves.

Eucalyptus leaves ⟶

Australian night parrots walk
around eating seeds.

Red kangaroos don't like to get too
hot. They graze on grass at night.

Rainforests are huge hot and steamy forests. They are home to lots of night animals.

Tree frogs have bright red eyes.

They open their eyes wide and jump to scare away attackers.

Cat-eyed snake

Flying foxes eat fruit. They find it by smelling it in the dark.

Fig cluster fruit

Tarsiers have huge eyes to help them find food at night.

Grasshopper

Some animals live in rivers during the day and come onto land at night.

Hippos stay cool in the water when it's hot and sunny.

At night, they come out onto the riverbank to eat grass.

Beavers climb onto land to eat trees, grass and other plants.

Caimans hunt animals that come to drink from the river.

Tapir

Caiman

At the end of the night, it starts to get light. Bats return to their sleeping places, called roosts.

Greater horseshoe bats

Other night animals go back into their dens or burrows.

Wolves

Owls find shady trees
to sleep in.

Great horned owl

Daytime animals begin to wake up.

Birds sing loudly to find partners.

Blackbird

Whistle!

European goldfinch

Chirp chirp!

European robin

Cheep!

Lizards get very cold at night.
They lie in the sun to warm up.

Collared lizard

Rabbits are awake early in the
morning. They find plants to eat.

The day gets brighter and warmer.
Lots of bugs wake up.

Dragonflies hunt for
other bugs to eat.

Shield bug

Bees and butterflies feed from flowers.

Monarch butterfly

Honey bee

Swallowtail butterfly

Some night animals are awake
during the day too.

Foxes look for food for their cubs.

Digital retouching by John Russell

First published in 2017 by Usborne Publishing Ltd., Usborne House, 83-85 Saffron Hill, London EC1N 8RT England. www.usborne.com Copyright © 2017 Usborne Publishing Ltd. The name Usborne and the devices ♀⊜ are Trade Marks of Usborne Publishing Ltd. All rights reserved. No part of this publication may be reproduced, stored in a retrieval system, or transmitted in any form or by any means, electronic, mechanical, photocopying, recording or otherwise without the prior permission of the publisher. First published in America 2017. AE.